# POSTERS:

## TURN-OF-THE-CENTURY

## CONTENTS

Published by
**CASTLE BOOKS**
A Division of
**BOOK SALES, INC.**
110 Enterprise Avenue
Secaucus, New Jersey 07094

# INTRODUCTION

During recent years, Art Nouveau and other turn-of-the-century styles have become immensely popular. The fragile, iridescent glass of Tiffany, Lalique, and Gallé; the exotic jewelry of Fabergé; the beautiful books of William Morris, with their stamped leather bindings and fine Gothic-revival illustrations; and most of all the posters of Mucha, Toulouse-Lautrec, Steinlen, and other artists have become objects to be admired and collected, and have drawn record crowds to auction houses.

Turn-of-the-century posters have, in fact, never been treated so impressively. When they first appeared in Paris and London they were pasted on the walls of buildings and on hoardings—the temporary walls made of wooden boards which are put up around construction sites. In short, they were not works of art, but advertisements. In the period known as the *Belle Epoque*, or Golden Era, at the end of the nineteenth century, advertising posters, though not a new invention, were suddenly proliferating rapidly, and blending fine art with commercial art in an entirely new way.

Designed to attract attention, to carry a message attractively and persuasively to even the most casual viewer, they were primarily a means of communication, rather than an expression of an artist's feelings. Posters usually contained both pictorial and written elements; and in a successful poster, the drawn image and the written word were well balanced, to produce the best possible effect and convey their information clearly.

Posters of a sort had been used as mere advertisements since the 1700s; they were not considered a pure art form. Nevertheless, toward the turn of the century, artists began to exercise considerable creativity and skill to persuade the public to buy magazines, cigarettes, and liquors, and, as they brought the principles of fine art to their commercial work, they also persuaded the public that the posters themselves were beautiful in their own right. People began to remove them from public displays to hang in their own homes, then to buy them, finally to write books about them, until they gradually became a fashion.

It is impossible to speak of the decade before the turn of the century, and of the art of the poster, without looking at the style known as Art Nouveau, a style marked by a delicate, swirling line, a strong sense of design, and a glorification of the feminine and sensuous. Art Nouveau design is based on naturalistic forms: especially the tendrils and curves of plant shapes. It is close to nature in its inspiration but abstracts from it, using repeated patterns and stylized images to create beautiful, rather elegant pictures. Thus, an artist might be inspired by an iris or a lily to draw a floral motif with soft, heavy lines, graceful curves, and delicate coloring—like the flower—but might make his lines so fluid and intertwined that no specific flower could be distinguished in the overall pattern. Such shapes and images appeared everywhere: in designs for furniture and wallpaper, jewelry and silverware, and even doorknobs and subway entrances. The style appeared mostly in the decorative and commercial arts—including poster and book design—and was less influential in the fine arts of painting and sculpture. The movement owes its basis to several influences: the work of William Morris in England; the development of new technologies for producing art, such as lithography; and, perhaps most important, the sudden appearance of Japanese art in the West, imported after Japan began to trade with Europe in the late 1850s. The opening of Japan to the West made Japanese-style objects very popular in Europe; westernized versions of Japanese ornaments enjoyed a great vogue; people decorated rooms with fans, brocaded silks, and screens, and began to collect the exquisite Japanese color-woodblock prints, called *ukiyo-e*, which had never been seen in the Occident before. The fine qualities of Japanese art impressed western artists, who soon went beyond this popularization to absorb the elements of oriental design: the large areas of flat color, the contour line, the two-dimensional surface composition and lack of depth-perspective—elements which lent themselves readily to the newly discovered printing techniques. The assimilation of Japanese ideas of design altered the direction of European art radically, as its influence extended to the work of the most skilled and brilliant artists: Van Gogh, Gauguin, Bonnard, and Toulouse-Lautrec in France, Whistler and Beardsley in England, Klimt in Vienna, and others.

The turn of the century marked the beginning of the popular age, in which the strict division of social classes began to break down. The decades just before and after 1900 not only saw radical advances in technology, industry, and mass communications, but also witnessed massive changes in the economic and political order. The power of the common man—the "man in the street"—grew very great in this period, and with it came a new economic market. Partly in response to this market, a new focus for art developed. The formal, elegant creations of the French and British Art Academies were gradually abandoned in favor of paintings which showed people in relaxed poses, or engaged in commonplace and commercial activities. The new art form of the poster was almost entirely concerned with everyday subjects. These bold, colorful posters had widespread appeal to all classes of society when they first appeared; the attraction has continued, for their popularity has never been greater than it is today.

## JULES CHERET

Chéret (1836-1932) is considered the father of modern poster technique. Born in Paris, he studied lithography, which was, at that time, a new method of reproducing colored designs cheaply. His studies of this revolutionary process took him to London, where he remained until 1866. Then he returned to Paris and set up his own shop, where he began printing theatrical posters done in a remarkable and innovative style. Chéret used lithographic techniques to create lively, mobile images. His sense of design, his free-hand style, and his ability to incorporate written messages into his pictures smoothly were skills that combined to produce posters which attracted the attention and interest of the viewer immediately. Like Toulouse-Lautrec after him, Chéret was influenced by the Post-Impressionists and by Japanese prints. He used more detail than was usual in posters at the time, and depicted inviting, unframed scenes of figures caught in mid-action. Chéret's posters contained an unusually large amount of lettering, which brought the element of advertising in his designs into prominence. His principles of good poster design influenced Toulouse-Lautrec, and paved the way for the other poster artists of his time. Although rather bold in style at the turn of the century, Chéret later turned to a milder, impressionistic treatment of his subjects.

*Paris Courses* (1890)
Chéret typically fills this poster with both pictorial images and written text, managing to arrange all the elements without obscuring his message. Chéret was very successful as a poster "ad man" and created such major posters as the one for the opening of the Cabaret Moulin Rouge. In *Paris Courses,* he uses a limited range of colors and a strong line to convey action, and sets one of his cabaret ladies on horseback to connect the gaiety and excitement of the dance hall with that of the racetrack. The lady on the horse is caught in mid-stride, placing the viewer at an unusual perspective. Chéret was the first poster artist to use this almost photographic trick: placing his figures — usually cheerful women — in stop-action scenes. In capturing this atmosphere, he was aided by the flexibility of the lithography medium, which permitted some of the rough quality of brush-painting to appear in the finished print. Although his posters do not have the serpentine lines and stylized forms of later artists', it was Chéret's brilliant sense of design which was to inspire Art Nouveau.

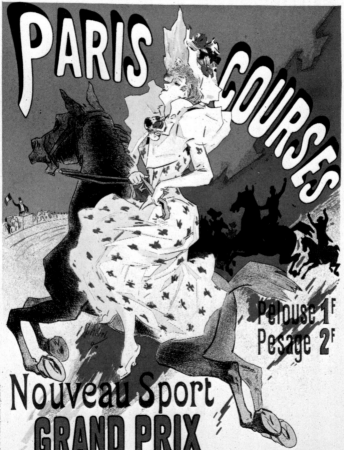

## HENRI DE TOULOUSE-LAUTREC

Toulouse-Lautrec (1864-1901) came from an old, wealthy, and titled family. Two bad falls in adolescence and a genetic bone deficiency left him crippled, with stunted legs and a grotesquely deformed body. He moved to Paris when he was eighteen, and there began to study art formally. Frustrated by his teachers' rigid academicism, he abandoned classical training for the bohemian nightlife of the music halls and cabarets of Montmartre. He was fascinated by the work of Manet, Degas, and Van Gogh, and was greatly influenced by both the Japanese prints which were in vogue in Paris at that time, and by the Impressionism which was appearing in the art galleries of the city. He designed his first poster in 1891—the startling poster for the Cabaret Moulin Rouge. Compared with the rather pretty posters of Chéret and Steinlen, the harsh caricatures and stark figures in Lautrec's advertisements for the dance halls, cabarets, circuses, and bistros of Paris created a sensation. Lautrec spent many hours in these places, sketching the can-can dancers, the drinkers, and the audiences. His rather morbid curiosity led him to murder trials, hospitals, race courses, and sporting events, where in endless drawings he captured the gestures and attitudes of the people around him. His style was loose—the opposite of such precisionists as Mucha, Grasset, and Beardsley—and his mastery of lithographic technique complete. The expertise of his work rests on the surely drawn line—a freehand arabesque that describes the central figures of his drawings and posters, and which was a mark of the emerging Art Nouveau style. His gift, however, lay in his often cruel and satiric truthfulness, in his ability to catch fleeting expressions of emotion and momentary gestures of vulnerability in his characters.

### *Moulin Rouge (La Goulue)* (1891)
Lautrec, a regular patron of the Moulin Rouge, was asked by the cabaret to do an advertisement for its official opening in 1889. The characters in the picture were well known to him: La Goulue ("The Glutton"), the dancer famed for her wild can-can and shown here at the center of the poster; Valentin, known as "The Boneless One", La Goulue's favorite dance partner, shown in silhouette in the foreground; and the crowd of admiring customers who gather about the dance floor, drawn in a solid black silhouette in the background. The influence of Japanese prints is evident in the artist's use of areas of flat color and in the strong, calligraphic contour lines. Lautrec's hallmarks—his sketchy line and hazy, speckled colors—can be seen here in places; in later posters they became more pronounced.

## THEOPHILE-ALEXANDRE STEINLEN

Steinlen (1859-1923) was born in Switzerland, where he studied art at Lausanne and later became active as a textile designer in Mulhause. In 1882 he arrived in Paris, where he worked as an illustrator for the journals *Mirliton, Assiette au Beurre, Chat Noir,* and *Gil Blas*, for which he produced over four hundred lithographs. As an artist he was not merely a commercial success, but showed great sensitivity toward his subject matter. Besides illustrating advertisements for a variety of products, Steinlen was famous for his posters of cabaret and music hall performers. Perhaps the most noteworthy of these is one done for the French singer Yvette Guilbert's performances at the cabaret Les Ambassadeurs, executed in 1894. Guilbert preferred Steinlen's poster to another famous version, done by Toulouse-Lautrec, in which the artist distorted her features and figure, making her appear thin and bony to the point of freakishness. The two artists are often compared, although Steinlen's poster art, drawn with the same bold simplicity as Lautrec's, is marked by an air of sweetness and a quieter mood. However, his later work for the journals, like that of Lautrec, became increasingly satirical and critical of society. Steinlen, too, often drew genre scenes of the working class, capturing day-to-day life in Paris with a simple, endearing style. He was very fond of animals, especially cats, and often included them in his posters. Steinlen's cats proved so popular, in fact, that they became a trademark of his work.

### *Motocycles Comiot* (1889)

The influence of Toulouse-Lautrec is evident here in Steinlen's use of color and his graceful, wavering lines. Like Lautrec, Steinlen loved to apply colors with a grainy, paint-spattered texture to achieve variations in tone. The medium of lithography, which gave his posters a soft, slightly hazy light, was well suited to this loose technique. The lightness of mood helps to bring the message of this poster across to the viewer. The young woman on her new machine seems to float above the peasant farmers and the flock of geese that surround her. She is colorfully dressed in the style of the day, and contrasts brightly with the dull brown and cream shades of the background. Steinlen's well-conceived poster ads were among the most charming of the period. Here, he has drawn the startled geese and smiling woman with his usual gentle wit.

## PIERRE BONNARD

The reputation of Pierre Bonnard (1867-1947) rests largely on his paintings. One of the leading artists of the Post-Impressionist movement, he painted studies brilliant in design and color, rainbow-hued canvases which owe much to the Impressionism of Monet and to Japanese prints. Bonnard was interested in color to the point of obsession; it is therefore something of a surprise that his background and early training were in decorative art, illustration, and poster design. He had first planned to be a lawyer, but later enrolled in the School of Fine Arts in Paris. He went on to study at the Académie Julian, where the younger and more avant-garde painters of Paris gathered. There he met Paul Serusier, Maurice Denis, and Edouard Vuillard, among others; together these five young artists formed a group called the *Nabis*, or "Prophets," and painted pictures with wild, dazzling colors and symbolic rather than strictly representational images. The *Nabis* had close ties to the literary and artistic movement called Symbolism, which was popular in Paris at the turn of the century, but Bonnard, who was neither an academic nor an intellectual painter, approached his art as a designer and decorator. He was a skilled lithographer, and, like many of the great poster artists of the period, his posters show a fine sense of two-dimensional design. His flat surfaces derive from Japanese art, and his wavering lines and strong silhouettes are reminiscent of those of Toulouse-Lautrec. From 1890 to about 1904 he did illustrations for magazines and books, and posters for theaters and publishers. By 1905, his interest in color, and in the problems of perception and representation, had led him away from applied art, into the stricter medium of pure painting. He did not return to lithography or engraving until the 1920s. Bonnard's work always bordered on abstraction, and even in his earliest efforts, his concern for composition, unmodelled shapes, and expressive line is apparent. Like Lautrec, Bonnard is one of those rare artists who are masters of both pure art and decorative design.

### La Revue Blanche (1894)
*La Revue Blanche* was a Symbolist periodical to which Bonnard contributed work for a time. The figures in this unusual poster design are slightly mysterious, in keeping with the Symbolist idea that an image in art was "an idea clothed in a sensitive form" rather than a realistic picture of an object. Bonnard never embraced the principles of Symbolism fully, but this poster has more in common with those principles than with the more frivolous and ornamental tastes of Art Nouveau. Here, two figures are posed in front of a magazine stand filled with copies of *Le Revue Blanche*. The tall, fashionably dressed woman also holds a copy of the journal. The poster is executed in tones of brown, tan, and grey, and is a study of silhouettes.

## ALPHONSE MUCHA

Alphonse Marie Mucha (1860-1939), a Czechoslovakian-born artist, was raised in a strict Roman Catholic environment, and the religious tradition of rich decoration was later to play an important part in his art. Mucha's style is marked by a wealth of luxurious detail; he used muted colors, gold leaf, complicated and delicate patterns, and intricately intertwined lines — the whole overlaid with a feeling of mystic ritual. As a young man he studied at the Prague Academy of Fine Arts, and later, under the sponsorship of Count Khuen, at the Munich Academy. He came to Paris in 1887 and worked under Lefebvre, Boulanger, and Laurens. Mucha combined the principles of theatrical design he had learned in Prague with the classical technique taught to him in Paris, and developed from them the elaborate Art Nouveau style for which he is known. In 1889, at the Paris World Exhibition, Mucha first saw Japanese prints, which, with their flat surfaces and graceful, curving outlines, influenced him deeply. He gradually incorporated those elements into his own art. In 1892 he executed his first lithographs. In 1894, almost by chance, he received his first commission to design a poster—for Sarah Bernhardt's *Gismonda*. Thus began a lifelong collaboration with the celebrated actress, who was so delighted with his initial work that she immediately contracted Mucha for six years of poster, set, and costume designs for some of her plays. The posters of Mucha's mature style were the ultimate expression of Art Nouveau with their sinuous lines, subtle coloring and glorification of the feminine ideal. While the influence of Japanese prints and of the poster artist Eugène Grasset as well as the Baroque churches of his childhood can be seen in his style, it was his association with Bernhardt that molded his art.

### *Job* (1898)

In this poster advertising a brand of cigarette papers, Mucha exhibits the most characteristic elements of his art: flowing lines, subtle colors, rich patterns, and the mysterious, goddesslike central figure of a woman. Here, the woman's hair looks almost abstract, its entwined tendrils curling like some exotic underwater plant. The word "JOB" — the brand name of the cigarette papers — is partially obscured by her head, and the cigarette she holds in her hand, ostensibly the subject of the poster, is clearly much less important than she is: the success of this poster as an advertisement depends on its attractiveness to the viewer, rather than the clarity of its message. Mucha became one of the leading artists of the Art Nouveau movement; indeed, his designs are so closely associated with the delicate Art Nouveau style that it is often referred to as *le style Mucha*.

## AUBREY BEARDSLEY

Of all the Art Nouveau artists, Aubrey Beardsley (1872-1898) is the best known and most esoteric. His sudden appearance in the art world in 1893, his tremendous notoriety both in that world and in English society, and his abrupt death at twenty-five from tuberculosis have lent his life an aura of the exotic. Noted for his draftsmanship, and use of contrasts of black and white, Beardsley took the principles of Art Nouveau, and the ideas of William Morris, and developed from them a style which is instantly recognizable. In 1893, Malory's tale of medieval chivalry, *Le Morte d'Arthur*, was published with 548 black-and-white line-block illustrations by Beardsley. These prints show Morris' influence in their floral borders and heavily decorated pages, but Beardsley also used asymmetrical designs, an irregular layout, and extremely dramatic contrasts of black, white, and patterned areas. The book caused a sensation in London. Beardsley, then twenty years old, and working in an insurance office, had no formal art training at all, but after the publication of *Le Morte d'Arthur*, he began to work professionally as an artist. Because he lived such a short time and had such a rapid rise to fame, it is almost impossible to isolate the artistic elements which influenced his style. He admired Japanese art, with its sinuous line, and the Renaissance richness of Pre-Raphaelites such as Burne-Jones. Beardsley led a mercurial life, alternately extolled and condemned by publishers, other artists, and his public. In the six years of his maturity, he produced an enormous volume of work: erratic, flawlessly drawn, and tinged with a macabre quality. He did many illustrations and poster designs for English magazines, theaters and publishers, and in 1894 became art editor of a newly formed journal, *The Yellow Book*. A man of many whims and eccentricities, Beardsley delighted in offending the public and transgressing the standards of propriety in both his art and his conduct. His effect on other artists at the turn of the century was atomic. As one contemporary artist said: "Every two-penny half-penny town had its 'Beardsley Artist' and the larger cities simply teemed with them."

### *Ali Baba – Cover Design for "The Forty Thieves"*
In this relatively late drawing, Beardsley's draftsmanship and sense of design have coalesced. He balances long, pure lines with exacting detail. Minuscule beads of ink sparkle against large areas of flat black and white. In the long curves of the figure's robes and in the delicacy of his features, we can detect the Art Nouveau style, but Beardsley's methods hold the elements of this drawing in a fine tension between decoration and abstract design.

*Reproduced Courtesy of the Fogg Art Museum, Harvard University, Cambridge, Massachusetts

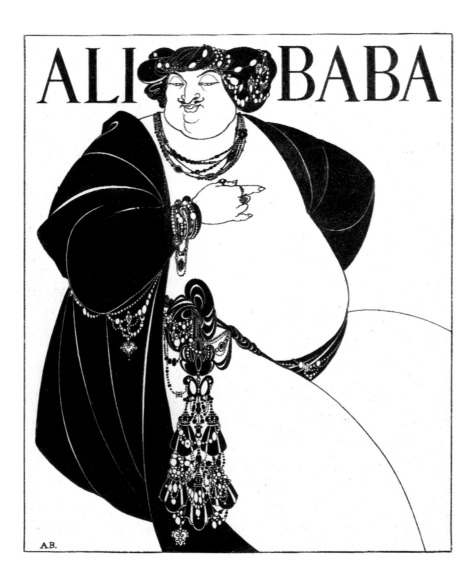

## THE "BEGGARSTAFFS"
(James Pryde and William Nicholson)

The English painters William Nicholson (1872-1949) and James Pryde (1886-1941), were known as the Beggarstaffs, or the Beggarstaff Brothers, although they were not really brothers at all, but brothers-in-law and close friends. They worked together as poster designers in England, and because both were fine academic painters with reputations to maintain, they took a pseudonym for their commercial work. Both had studied in Paris, at the famed Académie Julian, where Bonnard and other avant-garde artists of the turn of the century had worked. When they returned to England, they collaborated on a number of poster designs which, though more admired today than they were at the time, were nevertheless quite influential among commercial artists in Britain. Their technique was simple and unusual: they made paper cutouts, almost like silhouettes, and pasted them onto colored boards in collages which were then printed photographically. These first posters were designed so that the lettering could be added later, generally also in paper cutouts. Their style is unique, almost completely opposite to that of their contemporaries in the Art Nouveau movement. It is remarkable to think that they were working at the same time, in the same place, and in the same field as Aubrey Beardsley, whose hallmark is elaborate detail. The Beggarstaffs were geniuses of layout and design. Their work reflects the purity and elegance of Japanese art, especially in their use of large patches of blank color. They severely limited the range of colors and lines in their posters, producing effective advertisements which struck the viewer forcefully and immediately.

### *Don Quixote* (1896)
This ad for the Lyceum Theatre's production of *Don Quixote* uses lettering designed by the artists themselves. Its extreme economy of design made it as unpopular at the time of its creation as it is popular today. The poster was never used, perhaps because the public found it difficult to understand. Like Bonnard's *Revue Blanche* poster, it is a study in silhouette and in artful, abstract design. Solid white areas are set against solid black; the figure of Don Quixote is described in terms of shadow and light, and the unity of the picture is maintained by a series of thin lines: the curve of the ground, the Don's lance, the blades of the windmill. The poster uses what is known as "negative space" to very good effect. That is, the areas of space around the main objects in the picture are as important visually as the objects themselves. Although other turn-of-the-century poster artists had a talent for using this sophisticated device—notably Beardsley, Mucha, and Toulouse-Lautrec—the Beggarstaffs were its masters.

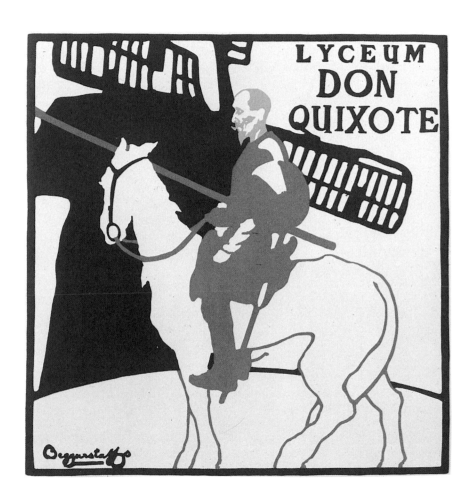

## LOUIS RHEAD

Louis Rhead (1857-1926), who was born in England, grew up in an artistic family. His father worked as an artist in a pottery factory, and his brother was a member of the English Society of Painter-Etchers. At thirteen, the young Rhead was able to go to Paris, where he studied under Boulanger, later finishing his studies under Paynter and Leighton at the School of South Kensington in London. Rhead then worked for *Cassell's Magazine* as a designer of book jackets and posters; as a result he was invited to New York in 1833 to work for D. Appleton & Co., a New York publishing house. He made New York his home, but from 1891 to 1894 returned to Europe to study in London and Paris. It was in Paris that he met Eugène Grasset, and first began poster work. The Wunderlich Gallery in New York gave Rhead a one-man exhibition in 1895 and another show followed in 1897 at the Salon des Cent in Paris. He was awarded a gold medal at a poster exhibition in Boston in 1904 and one at the World Exhibition in St. Louis the same year. Rhead created many posters for *Scribner's* magazine and the *Journal* and *New York Sun* newspapers, among others.

**The Sun** (1894)
This simple but very appealing advertisement gives us a hint of Art Nouveau in the swirling lines of the woman's clothes and the background landscape. The flowers and trees that Rhead uses here are a common motif in Art Nouveau as well. But Rhead's unusual color combinations and his use of full scenes with detailed backgrounds make his art distinctive. The influence of William Morris' Arts and Crafts movement, an English forerunner of Art Nouveau which incorporated themes from medieval art and used a strict formula for layout and design, are visible in the figure's long red robe and the formal composition.

20

## WILL BRADLEY

Will Bradley (1868-1962) was a cartoonist, illustrator, decorator, and architect. One of the leading American poster artists of the turn of the century, his facility in the graphic arts earned him the nickname "The American B," a reference to the great English graphic artist, Aubrey Beardsley. Born in Boston, Bradley received his first formal artistic education from his father, who worked as a cartoonist for the *Daily Item*, a local Massachusetts newspaper. In 1880, Bradley began a long career as a journalist, working for the *Iron Agitator*. He continued his journalistic pursuits until 1887, when he decided to move to Chicago to work for the prestigious printers, Knight and Leonard. By the 1890s, he had become an independent designer, working for *Harper's* and other magazines. He established his own studio, and produced theater posters as well as commercial advertisements. By 1895 he was back in Boston, where he published *Bradley: His Book, A Monthly Magazine Devoted to Art, Literature, and Printing*. In 1915, he began working for the newspaper magnate William Randolph Hearst, acting as art supervisor to a film series produced by Hearst. By 1920, he was head art supervisor of the Hearst magazines and newspapers. In 1954, Bradley was awarded a gold medal by the American Institute of Graphic Arts. Will Bradley's posters compare favorably with the best of the French and English poster designers of his generation. While Aubrey Beardsley set a formulative example, Bradley developed his own style of bold and elegant poster design, relying, like Beardsley, on sharp contrasts of black and white for strong visual impact. In addition to his graphic work, Bradley designed three houses for his family, revealing an interest in architecture influenced by the school of Glasgow and the work of Frank Lloyd Wright. He died at the age of ninety-four in Short Hills, New Jersey.

### *Victor Bicycles* (1896)

The influence of Beardsley on Will Bradley's work is evident in this advertisement for the Overman Wheel Co. Bradley's own embellishments on the severe linear style of Beardsley can be seen in the softly drawn white flowers of the poster's background. A deep purple tone surrounds the typical cold black and white of the forms. There is an elegant and airy quality surrounding the product to be merchandised that reveals Bradley's subtle skill as a graphic artist. The bicycle, in particular, is drawn in a graceful, somewhat stylized manner.

VICTOR BICYCLES

OVERMAN WHEEL CO.

## WILLIAM CARQUEVILLE

Although he studied in Paris for a brief time, Will Carqueville (1871–1946) lived in Chicago for most of his life. He founded his own lithographic press there, and designed posters for *Lippencott's* as well as other American literary magazines. His style was somewhat influenced by another American poster artist, Edward Penfield. In the United States, as in Europe at this time, literary magazines flourished, and several—*Harper's, Lippencott's, Scribner's,* and *The Atlantic Monthly* in particular—helped to popularize the current style of poster design, associating it with the cultural tastes of the day. Carqueville's work is classically American: clean, stylish, simple, and direct. American artists tended to be influenced by the British more than by the ornate and flamboyant French Art Nouveau. With the exception of Will Bradley and a few others, the Americans were not typically Art Nouveau at all. Their work was more realistic, still highly decorative, but not filled with the swirling abstract flowers of Mucha or Beardsley. Rather, they retained the graceful outlines and flat areas of color which had originally been inspired by Japanese prints.

*Lippencott's* (1895)
Carqueville, like many of the American poster artists, was a fine colorist. His *Lippencott's* poster depends for its effectiveness on sharp contrasts of bright colors—green, purple, red, and yellow—and simple, clear lines. This is an understated drawing, neither extremely ornamental nor filled with complicated lettering. It avoids the usual Art Nouveau devices of curlicue and pattern, relying instead on its sure design and cheerful brightness to attract the eye.

LIPPINCOTT'S
The Lady of Las Cruces
COMPLETE
LIPPINCOTT'S
MAY
WILL CARQUEVILLE

## ALEJANDRO DE RIQUER

Until the 1890s, Spanish posters lagged far behind their French and English counterparts in quality. They were mostly rough and garish advertisements for bullfights, with little artistic merit. But in the decade before the turn of the century, Spain produced a number of talented artists, most of whom were heavily influenced by French Art Nouveau. Among these, one of the best was Alejandro de Riquer Inglada (1856-1920), a nobleman who was the son of the Marques de Benavent. De Riquer had at first studied engineering in Barcelona, but quickly abandoned that career in order to enroll in the Barcelona School of Fine Arts. In 1874 he went to Rome, and spent time in Paris and London as well, perfecting his painting style. He returned to Spain a few years later, and became interested in book design. He later began to design posters, and his work, which reflects French Art Nouveau taste (especially the style of Mucha), is at the forefront of the Spanish School. Catalonia, and its capital city of Barcelona, became the artistic center of Spain at the turn of the century; De Riquer became one of the leaders of the new style, working in many media: painting, graphics, illustrations, and stained glass, as well as poster art. Although early in his career his paintings had been influenced by primitive and naive decoration, later his posters became richer in ornament, and more complex. He admired the posters of Grasset as well as Mucha, and traces of both men's styles appear in his work.

***Poster for the Third Barcelona Exhibition of Fine and Industrial Arts*** (1895)
This was one of De Riquer's first major poster designs. Its publication brought him much praise and established his reputation as an artist of more than merely imitative skill. His interest in Mucha can be seen in his use of gilded, Byzantine motifs—especially the mosaic-like pattern surrounding the poster's headline. The picture also has a Pre-Raphaelite flavor: the two ladies holding the emblems of the fine and applied arts might be Muses. They are dressed in medieval garb and drawn against a medieval-style floral background. The poster is marked by clear, easily read lettering (some of it also in a Gothic style), the written text gracefully incorporated into the overall design.

## G.M. MATALONI

Throughout its history, Italy had a tradition of fine opera posters and, at the turn of the century, a host of brilliant poster artists. Of these, Adolfo Hohenstein, Leopoldo Metlicovitz, and G.M. Mataloni were among the best. All three worked for the Milanese printers G. Ricordi and Co., a firm which pioneered lithography and other advanced printing techniques in Italy and encouraged the development of Italian Art Nouveau — called *Stile Liberty*, or Liberty Style — by inviting such artists as Mataloni to work with them under contract. The Italian poster artists excelled at many of the techniques which best characterized Art Nouveau design: superb draftsmanship, dramatic modelling of forms through color contrasts and intensive lighting, and a general air of grace. *Stile Liberty*, although derived from Art Nouveau, differed from its French counterpart in several respects. The Italians tended to rely less on abstract decorative patterns and fantastic scenes. They were known for their imaginative lettering; and since each artist was responsible not only for the pictures, but also for the text of his posters, this was very important. Little is known about Mataloni's life aside from his reputation as a skillful and dramatic artist of opera and advertising posters for Ricordi. He often used allegorical figures — generally young women — to symbolize the objects or ideas his posters were promoting.

*Incandescenza a Gas* (1895)
Mataloni's advertisement for a company that manufactured gas lights is a good example of the Art Nouveau idiom used in an unusual way. All the typical elements of ornamentation and decoration are here, but used to illustrate an unexpected theme: the incandescent element of the gas lamp. As is common in turn-of-the-century posters, the main object in this advertisement is a smiling woman. In one hand she holds a sunflower — a symbol of natural light; the other hand gestures to a gas mantle — a source of artificial light. Mataloni has drawn a border of curling floral forms around the poster, but upon close inspection we see that they are gas pipes and pieces of plumbing, subtly transformed into the tendrils and stems of flowers. Even the glowing gas mantle shines like a star. Art Nouveau artists were interested almost exclusively in elegant naturalistic motifs. Here Mataloni has cleverly turned a mechanical subject into a whimsical, allegorical picture.

## JOSEPH SATTLER

As a young man, Sattler (1867-1931) studied art at the Munich Academy; later he became a professor at the School of Arts and Letters in Strasbourg, and then, in 1896, settled permanently in Berlin. Germany at this time was much influenced artistically by a movement developing in Vienna and southern Bavaria, especially in Munich. There, and somewhat later in Berlin, a renaissance was occuring in the decorative and applied arts, and a new style, parallel to French Art Nouveau was emerging. The design revolution in Germany and Austria had some ties with France, and more with Belgium, but, on the whole, was less concerned with the ideal of feminine beauty, was not as heavily influenced by Japanese art, and had more in common with the logical geometry of the early abstract artists. There was strong emphasis on flat two-dimensionality, geometrical ornament and pattern. The Vienna Secession, as the movement was called, included such fine artists as Gustav Klimt and Egon Schiele, as well as furniture- and interior-designers, architects, textile designers, and many other applied artists. Sattler, primarily a book illustrator, discovered the new style while in Berlin, and incorporated elements of it into his own work.

### *Pan* (1895)

As in America and England, a vogue for avant-garde literary and cultural magazines sprang up in Germany at the turn of the century. The magazine *Pan* was founded in Berlin in 1895. Sattler's cover design for it is a striking example of the German version of Art Nouveau. Although strongly influenced by the early Vienna Secession, this poster still retains many elements typical of the more classic Art Nouveau style. A familiar emphasis on long, curling lines and flower images is apparent here, but Sattler has added a slightly eerie quality to his design: out of a large white flower made of curling pages of paper rise three long stamens which spell out the word "PAN"; four more, in red, form the date "1895." In the background, Pan, the god of forests and wild gardens, rises from the grass, a mysterious, secretive smile on his face. The poster contains a strong element of Symbolism—an artistic movement which combined Art Nouveau style with exotic, symbolic images and an air of esoteric spirituality.